What Is My PATH?

Francis Lukewood

PARTRIDGE

To order additional copies of this book, contact
Toll Free +65 3165 7531 (Singapore)
Toll Free +60 3 3099 4412 (Malaysia)
orders.singapore@partridgepublishing.com

www.partridgepublishing.com/singapore

CONTENTS

CHAPTER I: HEAD IN THE CLOUDS

CHAPTER II: A RUDE AWAKENING

CHAPTER III: THE STAGE OF DOUBT

CHAPTER IV: FINDING MY PATH

Chapter I

Head In The Clouds

The Dreams Of A Young Kid

As a kid, I was always told that I could be anything that I wanted to be. I know, right?, it's such a cliche line. But despite it being so cliche, I still believed it. I mean I was just some kid who knew nothing about the so called "real world" we live in. And so, having that belief in that saying, had me dreaming as big as I could possibly dream. I can still remember it like it was yesterday, when I was first asked by my relatives in the Philippines, what I wanted to be when I grew up and I said that I wanted to be a rockstar, and proceeded to pretend playing an electric guitar while screeching the tune that an electric guitar would make. I guess I chose the path of a rockstar, because of the thrill that came along with it. You know, jumping around on stage, while singing your original songs, screaming your lungs out, as you try to hype up the crowd. And just having an amazing time, as you play those guitar solos, that gets the crowd even more amped up than they already are.

I loved the idea of it so much, that one of my favorite shows back in my childhood was this show on Disney XD called "I'm In The Band". And if you haven't heard of it, it's about this teenage boy named Tripp Campbell, who's really, really good at guitar. And one day, we won a radio contest to have dinner with his favorite band called "Iron Weasel", and from there on out, he eventually became part of the band and they went on crazy adventures together. So yeah, that's the basic gist of it, and I used to watch that show every single day, after I came home from school. Thinking to myself, that it would be so awesome to live a life like that. It was a crazy and wild dream to have, seeing how the industry works nowadays, it's normally a one in a million chance for you to be an artist, let alone a rockstar and succeed. I mean don't get me wrong, I'm not saying that nobody can do it. But from what I've seen, only a few people ever make it big in that industry, and are labeled as rock legends till this day.

But like I said, at the time I didn't know any better. So, I continued to aspire to be like one, and it got to the point where I got a game called "Guitar Hero", and I was just in love with that game. Even though I was just bashing the buttons on the guitar controller, and I had no idea as to what I was doing. I was just enjoying the fact that I felt like I was a rockstar, jumping around to the sound of the music and pretending like I was on stage performing in front of thousands. But as I grew older, I seemed to completely forget about that so-called "dream", and never pursued it again. It was then, when I began to think logically about my dreams, and focused on exploring "realistic" job options.

Searching

And so, there I was again, wondering what career I could possibly pursue that could be more "realistic". But knowing my luck, I wasn't going to come up with anything, anytime soon. So, I decided to do some research on good career choices to pursue, as well as getting my parents opinion on it. And after searching far and wide for quite a while, I still came up with nothing. I know, you must be thinking, that this kid is literally looking at job options at this stage of his life?, well yup that's exactly what I did. I guess I was just either super bored at the time, or I was super keen to have everything in my life figured out, as early as possible. Come to think of it, I think it was definitely a mixture of two. But one thing for sure, whatever it is that drove me, it sure took me on one hell of a ride. But we'll get to that part soon enough. Anyways, days turned into weeks, and weeks turned into months, and I'm still clueless as to what type of job I would like to pursue now.

Then there came a day, where I had this crazy idea. This crazy idea revolved around changing the world for the better. Mainly, through helping people, and the only way that I thought I could do that was through being a doctor. Since I thought of helping as a way of curing and healing people of their illnesses and pains. To be honest, I thought that that was the only way for me to possibly help people. Hence the choices of subjects such as physics, biology, and chemistry in high school. I mean I did enjoy physics and biology quite a lot, but chemistry on the other hand was just a pain. Turns out it's not just about mixing chemicals and creating cool explosions. It's some of that, but mostly mathematical equations and formulas, which makes my head hurt just thinking about it.

It was quite the mental ride, but I managed to miraculously pull it off. I mean after all, I had no other choice in the matter, since I chose that path to begin with. Anyways a few tests and exams later, I was really enjoying these subjects and I thought to myself, why not get a job related to science?. I mean there are clearly a variety of extraordinary and amazing jobs out there. You could create and come up with unique discoveries, and advancements in technology, medicine, space, and beyond. I mean as they say, skies the limit. I found myself really enjoying the experiments we did in the science lab, especially the ones for biology and physics. Overall, I guess taking science was a pretty good choice after all. And I guess, someway, somehow, it'll get me one step closer to finding out what type of career I'd like to take in the future.

That One Teledrama

After some time, of watching countless romantic teledramas with my mom and siblings. I eventually stumbled upon this teledrama called "All of Me", and yes the theme song of it is the song All of Me by John Legend. Anyways, it was about this doctor, who was a great man, who wanted to genuinely help heal and tend to the illnesses of the people in his province. It's a pretty emotional show that's grounded in reality, with a hint of fantasy. But that show connected with me in a way that I never thought I would be connected to. It basically showed me how to genuinely care and love for the people around you, without having the need to ask for anything in return. Not only that, but it also showed me what it means to truly put oneself in the service of others.

This show further intrigued my interest, to the idea of becoming a doctor. It wasn't just about the salary, or status. It was mostly about how a job could teach you to have a sense of compassion, love, and concern towards people who are simply strangers. I mean caring for people who you know, is extremely hard enough, as it is. What more if it were strangers right?. But doctors somehow manage to do it on a daily basis. It made me realize that doing a job is more than just having the credentials, knowledge, and skill. It's about caring for the people who you serve. Whether it be your customers, patients, clients, and so on. The more we prioritize the people we serve, the better our service and approach to serving each and every one of them becomes.

And the more, I continued to watch the show, the more I began to learn not only about what it means to be a doctor, but also about life. It showed me how to love, It showed me how to care, it showed me how to trust, it showed me how to go after what you love, it showed me that if your passionate about something, you'll be able to succeed in it, no matter what obstacles, trials, hurdles, and challenges life throws at you. But most importantly, it showed me that everyone deserves a second chance, and when we do get that second chance we should make the most out of it.

Walking The Path

I was overjoyed and excited to embark on this new path that I've set out for myself. I told myself that I'll work extra hard, and be the best I could possibly be. And so I did, I studied every day and night. Doing my best in all my homework and tests, trying to get the highest marks in class. But of course, all of this didn't happen overnight. It took me a while to do it properly, and get into the habit of doing it day in and day out. I must admit, it was quite challenging and tiring at first, I mean how could you just stay there studying and working on assignments for hours on end without taking a break. I guess that's why I would always get so sleepy, even though it was just like 8 or 9 pm. But at the time, it was worth it, since I slowly began seeing the results, and I was happy with them.

I began to get this rush of adrenaline and satisfaction, whenever I would get a high grade, or a good comment from my teachers on my work. And so, I began to constantly crave that feeling of adrenaline and satisfaction in every single task and work that I do. So, there I went, with many endless days of just focusing on school work. It was basically study in school, then study as soon as I get home, and then eat and sleep afterwards. It was a repetitive cycle, but it was a repetitive cycle that I was very comfortable with. And this cycle was working very well for me actually.

But as we know, no path in life is an easy one to walk on. There are going to be challenges, trials, and hurdles that are going to hurt or break us, and unfortunately for me I wasn't aware of that. All I knew was that, if I worked hard enough it would always pay off, and it did. But there came this time, where I didn't get the grades that I was hoping for, and I was just crushed. I could still remember it so clearly, as soon as I saw my grades, I ran to my grandfather's room, locked the door, and in a fit of shock and disappointment, broke down and cried. I just couldn't believe nor accept it. My mom and grandfather tried to make me feel better, but it didn't do much. And looking back at it now, I guess the thing that crushed me the most, at the time, was not the fact that I didn't get the highest marks, but it was the fact that I couldn't accept it. I was just constantly in denial, which made it hurt even more. But I guess it was just life teaching me a lesson, a painful one, but a lesson nonetheless. And it would just so happen to be something that I needed to learn, in order for me to keep moving forward in this path of mine.

Trial & Error

I was never one to succeed at the first try. I would always commit some mistake or error, that would ultimately lead me to failing. This honestly made every single thing I do ten times more frustrating. Since I would always have to go back to the drawing board, and try to figure out what went wrong. This would go on for days, weeks, months, even years, up until I finally get it right. It's a pain, but I guess the satisfaction of finally successfully completing something that you've worked so hard for, is what makes all the pain worth it. I had to deal with this in every single aspect of my life, from school and university with tests and assessments, to hobbies, and relationships as well.

I get it, everyone has their own way of learning and getting through obstacles and challenges. But I can't lie, it gets really draining. From the constant failures, self doubts, headaches, and heartaches, to the amount of time that's been put into that one specific thing, because if it still doesn't work out, despite the time and effort you've invested in it, then it will all be a waste of time. And as we know, the one thing you could never get back in this life, is time. The time spent with people, the time spent on fixing mistakes, the time spent on correcting your wrongs, the time spent on trying to rewrite the past.

Realizing this, just made me question myself yet again. I mean, is it really worth it spending the majority of your life, constantly correcting your mistakes. Just so that you could get it completely right, and then you'd have to do it again, and again, and again, for the rest of your life. It made me stop for a moment and ask myself, is this how you'd really want to live your life?, are you really willing to sacrifice the time you have on this?. And till this day, I never really got an answer to the question. So, I just keep my head down, continue to try, and try, until something eventually works.

Motivation

Now, if I really hated failing and constantly being put a step back from where I was, what is it that keeps me motivated to keep trying?. And the answer to that, is mainly based on the belief that whatever it is that I'm working on right, would eventually become something profitable, or impactful to the world in the future. It's having that thought in my mind when I wake up, and having it in mind when I go to sleep. It's kind of a form of deception in a way, if you think about it. Since it keeps me believing that whatever it is that I'm doing could possibly become a reality, instead of it remaining a dream. Even though this dream of mine might be completely bizarre or unrealistic in everyone else's eyes, on the other hand, it's completely in the realm of possibility in my eyes.

So, I guess you could say that I'm pretty much self motivated right? Well, not exactly. Mainly because people's support, specifically the support from my friends and family, are a major factor in my motivation to do things. That support served as an extra kick, to motivate me into continuing my hobbies, my passion projects, and anything work related overall. But apart from that it's mostly self-motivation, I mean at the end of the day, it's all up to me. Whether I want to do it or not, continue an existing project or scrap the whole thing and start over. At the end of the day, people and their thoughts are just a mere form of influence, and the only person who really decides whether we start, continue, or end something, is ourselves.

In my case, at the time, I chose to continue pursuing my dream of becoming a doctor. No matter how hard it was, no matter how draining or demotivating it was, I still chose to continue pursuing it. Despite the countless setbacks, failures, and self-doubt, I chose not to give up. Only because I saw myself, making a difference in the world, and in people as well. But little did I know that this would all change in a span of a year.

Things Are Looking Up

It was middle school, and I was so happy that I was continuing to see results of my work. I was finally seeing something good come out of all the constant studying, and work. I had been told by my teachers that I was doing good, and to keep it up. This continued to boost my confidence in my work and in myself. But of course there were times where I failed, and there were times where I didn't perform as well.   Nothing was ever completely perfect, I did have to fail and learn, again and again, but in the end after two or three attempts at it, I was able to successfully complete it.

I found myself not being as demotivated or discouraged by little failures here and there. Of course, I did feel bad whenever I couldn't get it right, but I didn't let that stop me from trying again. So, I guess you could say that I've started trying to accept the fact that I can't always be right. I mean I'm still not at that point yet, where I won't be completely phased by the failures or setbacks that I experience, but I'm trying. It's going to hurt, it's going to sting, and it's going to constantly play with my confidence, but if there's one thing I know for sure, it's that these challenges aren't going to keep me down.

I was still not fond of hearing criticisms, even though some of them were constructive. But I got to learn how to put my ego aside, and admit that I made a mistake or I was wrong in a certain area. This helped me make adjustments in work, where necessary. And this helped me learn a better way of phrasing certain information, improving on my delivery when it came to presenting a topic to an audience, and overall improving in areas that needed some tweaking. So, just that fact that I was able to allow myself to be open to making necessary adjustments and improvements, was a sign that I am growing, and that alone was a sign that things are looking up.

A Hopeful Guy

At this point in my life, I kind of felt like things were finally going my way, you know. I felt good, and I was happy. I could finally say that I was genuinely satisfied with my life. And it didn't stop there, this feeling continued for quite some time. I was glad that things were looking up for myself, and this feeling had me stressing and worrying a little bit less than usual. I began sleeping a bit longer, smiling a bit more, laughing a bit more, and just appreciating the little things in life.

Waking up everyday with a smile on my face, as the rays of the sun begin to hit my face. Looking at myself in the mirror, feeling proud, as I begin to see the hope in my eyes. I began to dress better, talk better, and feel better. Whether it was at school, hanging out with my friends, during our class lessons, or at home simply having a snack as I watch TV, or it could be something as simple as sitting on the chair, listening to music, as I drink a cup of coffee. And as time went on, I stepped back and chuckled a bit, as I realized that I was able to change for the better.

This new and hopeful spirit of mine, translated to the words I say, the things I do, and the people I talk to. At the time, I was really at an all time high. I was at the top of the mountain, enjoying the beautiful view of the bright blue skies, and feeling the cool breeze of the wind brushing through my face. Back then, if you were to tell me that I would one day, be able to constantly smile, laugh, and just enjoy every little thing about my life, without having to worry about anything going wrong, I would've thought you were crazy. But a few months later, here I am, at the top, and I never come down.

A Sense Of Clarity

Having my mind free from all the worries and stress, gave me the head space to properly think about what I really want in life. So, I started thinking about each aspect of my life, starting with the guy in the mirror. I began questioning myself again, but it felt different this time. I was doing it, for the sole purpose of my plan in life, not because I had no idea what I was doing. I just really needed to know what it is that I want to do or achieve in this life. Is it to gain a lot of money? Is it to have a job that has the most vacation time? Is it to travel around the world? Is it to have all the pleasures and luxuries that this world has to offer? Is it to help those who are suffering? Or is it to simply settle down, with a family of my own, and with some of my closest friends?.

Knowing myself, I was unable to come up with an answer to that question at the time. So, I thought about it constantly, each and every day and night. And as I went on with life, I miraculously started getting answers to each of the questions little by little. Through my friends, my family, my classmates, teachers, traveling, and exploring. With the thrill of traveling to and exploring a different place, with seeing the smiles and hearing the laughter of my classmates, with feeling the joy and comfort that comes with seeing my closest friends, with all the love that comes with being around my family, with the sentimental feeling of the thought of settling down with a family of my own, with all the interesting things that I've learned from my teachers, I've come to a conclusion that each and every one of them, are equally as important as the other.

Well I guess, that is one problem solved, now on to the next one, which is planning this all out in a way where I could achieve and experience each and every single one of these things, in the span of my lifetime. No matter how long my life may last, I only long for one thing now, and that is to achieve and experience every single one of these things that I've mentioned, before I die.

The Plan

Now, the planning begins. I figured that if I were to have the best chance to achieve everything that I planned to do, I should make a list. Just so that I could keep track of every single thing. Because I know myself to be a very forgetful guy, and the likelihood of me forgetting to do one of the many things that I've mentioned is very high. So, I noted every single one of my dreams, and the order in which I want to achieve them. And the list went a little something like this:

My Life's Bucket List

- Goal 1: Get a job that pays well
- Goal 2: Earn a lot of money
- Goal 3: Support my parents and siblings
- Goal 4: Travel to Spain
- Goal 5: Go Sky Diving

- Goal 6: Fall in love, with a beautiful girl
- Goal 7: Live in a big house with my friend and our siblings
- Goal: 8: Get a 1970's Dodge Charger
- Goal 9: Create an organization that helps out the less fortunate
- Goal 10: Settle down in a beautiful country, along with a family of my own

Huh?, just seeing it now, it's one hell of a checklist. I guess I have a lot of dreams, for a person my age. But no matter how big these dreams may seem, I never saw them as something impossible. I knew that deep inside my gut, I just needed to work hard and commit to whatever it is that I wanted to achieve, without getting distracted, and I could make all of these dreams a reality.

As for now, well I'm still at phase one. Since I'm still in school and all, I still have to find a job, and then work my way up to a position where I'll get paid a higher salary and so on, but in time, I'll get there. I just need to focus on trying to achieve them one by one. Being patient, when things don't turn out the way I want it too. Keep going, no matter what life throws at me.

Taking these dreams, as well as everything else in life, one step at a time. But most importantly, never giving up on any of these dreams of mine, no matter how hard pursuing them may be.

Keep Hustling

You have to work twice as hard as the other guy, you have to be better than the other guy, why are your grades or stats lower than usual? Are you even trying? Do you even want to succeed?. These are the types of things that I've been told, whenever my efforts never measured up, and whenever I've watched motivational videos. It annoys me sometimes, but it also keeps me in check. Despite all their words being so cliche, repetitive, and overrated, I still use it as a form of motivation, to help me get up every single day and feel like I want to conquer the entire world.

I guess even someone like me, needs a little motivation every now and then from somewhere. I mean, I've tried motivating myself for a while now, and it gets kind of exhausting sometimes. So yeah, I'm a stickler for motivational content. Whether it be from quotes, stories, movies, or music. I believe that, just having someone pumping you up, rooting for you, and supporting you, every single step of the way could really help someone tremendously. It could sometimes be the one thing that helps them in sky rocketing to their dreams.

And that's exactly what it's done for me. From all the motivational videos, talks, music, movies, and support from friends and family. All of It has helped me form this mindset, of hustling in every single thing that I do. It's what pushed me, and continues to push me to put my all into everything that I love. More importantly, it's what motivates me to keep moving forward. To the point where even if, I'm bombarded with a lot of challenges and trials along the way. I'll still have that drive to keep persevering, and keep hustling.

Chapter II

A Rude Awakening

Constant Failures

Lately, I've noticed that the more I continue to hustle, and push through the multiple bad days, and rough times. They just continue to keep piling up. It's like this never ending mountain of problems, that just keeps coming. I don't know if it's just a coincidence, or if life is purposely trying to make things even more difficult for me. Let's take this situation for example, I used to succeed a lot in things when I was younger. But as I grew up, I found that things just instantly became extremely harder. And knowing this now, it frightened me a bit. Knowing that my current efforts aren't enough anymore. But what actually scared me the most, was that I may no longer be able to bounce back from my failures and shortcomings.

This fear of failing and not measuring up, resurfaced once again, and it decided to stay for quite some time. So, I reverted to that person who was scared to try or give anything that's new a shot. Knowing well, that I would just instantly mess up and fail. It was very daunting, and I did not enjoy a single second of it. It was like I was confined in this box, which had been chained and sealed with a thousand locks. And every time, I would have the slightest feeling of trying out something new, knowing that it would work out, the fears, insecurities, and doubts start to creep in.

Now, as I progressed through this stage of self-doubt, I just found myself getting worse and worse with the passage of every single day. When it eventually reached the point of me constantly questioning myself again. Asking myself, after every missed opportunity, what went wrong? Why didn't you go for it? Why are you so scared? Why didn't you say it? Is this even me?. I literally allowed my own fears and self-doubt to take control of myself to the point where I'm left with nothing but uncertainty.

Living In Uncertainty

Ever since I've once again allowed myself to be controlled by my fears, I've been constantly on edge. I'm constantly second guessing everything I say or do. It's like whenever I'm conversing with someone on a certain topic or matter and I say something important or crucial to the conversation, immediately after saying it, I have these voices in my head saying things like, "that was so dumb", "you could've thought of something better to say", "why did you say that?", "that was so cheesy", and these things continuously revolve around my mind, while I'm talking to people.

In terms of the things I do, I've noticed that whenever I'm doing daily mundane things like let's say doing homework, washing dishes, or making a drink or something, I was constantly second guessing my actions, like after washing a plate, I immediately look back at that plate and continuously ask myself is this clean enough?, does it have some leftover food or stain left that I miss?, Is this drink too sweet?, why does this taste so bland?, why does this drink not taste as sweet or as tasty as it was before? Did I put in too much sugar? Did I not put any flavor in this drink?. And in terms of my work, I've second guessed answers that I've written for my assignments, thus causing me to overcomplicate and overextend answers that were otherwise fine for the question asked.

All of these questions just made me make these situations much worse. I mean, I dropped a few plates trying to rewash them. I completely ruined the taste and consistency of the drinks. And completely reforming and rephrasing my answers to the questions for my homework, to the point where I've written just a bunch of large, meaningless, and senseless paragraphs. So, not only did this fear stop me from trying out experiences and opportunities that would otherwise benefit me as a professional, and as a person in general, but it also made me constantly mess up in the things that I've been doing for my entire life.

Voices In My Head

I was so nervous, I was so confused. My mind was just filled with all these voices. Voices that tell me that I'm not enough, voices that tell me that I'm worthless, and it just continues to drive me insane. I wish I could just tell them to shut up, and leave me alone, but I can't. They're not coming from people, who I can just avoid and ignore, they're coming from within my mind, and that is something I have to live with on a daily basis. And the more I think about it, the more I give in to these voices saying that I'm pathetic, because I am. I mean, it's my mind yet I can't drown out these negative thoughts? It's my heart, but I can't help but feel these negative emotions. It just doesn't make sense at all now does it?.

I bet that as you're reading this, you're probably thinking that this guy's mentaly unstable, this guy isn't thinking straight, this guy is just overreacting, and you're probably right. I mean who in their right mind, would constantly listen and give in to so much negativity, let alone demotivate and derail themselves time and time again. But I guess every one of us does, every now and then. But I took this to an extreme, and sometimes I do actually wonder, if these voices are there in my mind, because I wanted them to be there. I mean I've hated myself for quite some time now, for never being enough, for always being the loser, for always being the one left behind, and for missing out on so many potentially great opportunities for myself. Simply because I was just too scared to go for it.

Maybe these voices are simply saying things that I've really wanted to say to myself for a long time. Maybe these voices are just a sign. A constant sign that remains there, for the sole purpose of reminding me to stop being afraid, to stop shying away, to stop giving into fear, to stop caring about what other people think, and to stop overthinking things for once, and just go for it.

Scrap That

With all the doubt that's surrounding my head right now, I feel like scraping my dream of becoming a doctor. Partially because I was doubtful if I could ever make it work with my skills, but it was mainly because I was doubtful whether I really wanted this. I was questioning myself, if this was truly what I wanted out of life. Is being a doctor what I really wanted to be? What if I wanted to become something else? And what if that, something else is still out there for me to find?. All these questions began to surround my mind, and for some odd reason, I knew the answer right away. And the answer was simply no. No, being a doctor is not what I really want to be, nor do I know what I want to be in the future. And if I'm being honest with myself, I haven't really properly thought it out yet.

The only reason as to why I keep coming up with these dreams of mine that I want to achieve, is simply because of how I'll be perceived by the people around me and people in general. I would be admired and adored by people, I would be famous and an icon to people I'd become a rockstar. Being a doctor on the other hand, would have people perceive me as a hero. A hero who's cured a lot of illnesses, and healed a lot of people from their physical pains. I mean, don't get me wrong, the reason as to why I wanted to become a doctor in the first place was so that I could help people. But I did see value and satisfaction in the attention and praise that I would get for my service.

But as time went on, I asked myself. Is this what you really want? The fame, the attention, and the praise?. I thought you wanted to be happy? Will getting that really make you happy?. Once again, the answer was no. Because in time, the craving for the attention and praise, would eventually take over. Instead of the intention of doing the job, simply because you enjoy and love doing it.

Just Go With The Flow

Now, being absolutely clueless on what path I wanted to take, I just decided to quit planning for a while and just went with the flow. I just felt as if I've been trying to plan the perfect life for myself, when I don't even really know what that looks like. All I really have are mere perceptions and opinions, of what a perfect life looks like for other people. But I really need to find out what a perfect life looks like for me. And I couldn't think of any other way to do that, than just going with the flow. At Least that way, I'll be able to genuinely experience things naturally, instead of constantly forcing myself to experience things that I think I would like. And I thought that experiencing things naturally will eventually lead me to finding out what experiences I enjoy the most, who are the people I want to have in my life, and of course, what do I really want to do for a living.

But this approach came with a price. That price being, that I would have to go with wherever life takes me. Be it an easy and less problematic path, or the complete opposite, being a path filled with problems, complications, and difficulties, every step of the way. But this time, I felt more prepared. Since I definitely knew what I was getting into, when I thought of taking this approach. And low and behold, that is exactly what happened. I went through a rollercoaster of situations and emotions, from positive and easy ones, to extremely difficult and negative situations. But if there's one thing that I didn't expect, was that taking this type of path and approach towards life, requires you to have extremely firm and strong faith in yourself, and the things happening around you.

Developing the mindset of, everything happens for a reason. Seeing the purpose of certain things happening, certain events taking place, and certain people entering or leaving your life, no matter how bad or good it may be. Because all of it is all building up to your end goal, to where you'll be at when you reach the finish line, to your destination after going through this long and winding journey called life.

Strange, But Nice

With every passing second, hour, and day. I've been growing quite laid back, not really thinking or worrying about anything. Simply watching things happen right before my very eyes, without having the need to control every little detail about every situation that occurs. It's quite nice, for a change. I've been just allowing myself to live for once. Talking to people, without having any hidden agenda. Just having a normal conversation, and trying to get to know each other, and asking how they are doing. Going out on small walks by myself, with absolutely no destination in mind. Just appreciating the beautiful scenery, as the cold breeze of wind blows by, and the birds begin to chirp.

After a while of walking, I decided to stop for a while and take a seat on the concrete floor. As I was seated, I closed my eyes and just listened to the sound of the waves crashing against the sea wall. While doing so, I simply took a deep breath, and for a moment I felt this weight lifted off my chest. As I opened my eyes, I saw a bright and shining scenery before me, as the waves began to calm down, and the sun's radiant rays began to reflect on the surface of the still water. It was so relaxing and calming, that I could stay there for hours on end, just looking at the view.

But at last it was getting late, and it was time for me to head back home. So, I took one last look at the place with a smile, and left. As I returned home, I went to my room and got changed, then had my dinner, checked my assignments, chatted with some friends, and went to bed. But while I was laying down, I was having trouble sleeping. I tried watching something to help me fall asleep, but that didn't work. Then, I tried listening to some slow songs, because that usually helps. But sadly it didn't help at all this time. So, I just removed my headset and switched off my phone altogether. Then I just closed my eyes, and envisioned myself sitting on the ledge of that sea wall, listening to the sound of the waves again, and what do you know, it worked.

A Safe Haven

From that day onward, I would always go for a walk to that specific place whenever I would reach home from school, or in the afternoon on a weekend. Whenever I was sad, whenever I was mad, whenever I was going through a phase I couldn't understand, whenever I was troubled, whenever I was anxious, and whenever I just wanted to get away from reality for a while. For some reason, just listening to the sound of the waves and taking a deep breath, always managed to calm me down. Even without having the need to scream or cry, I was able to release all of my worries, pains, and sorrows.

I would stay there, watching the view, as people would be running, cycling, having picnics, and enjoying the view as well. Seeing the smiles and laughs of those people around me made me smile. It made me feel protected in a way from everything that was going on.

It was the first time that I felt safe, just by being alone. But as the sun begins to set, and the day slowly comes to an end. I had made my way back home, and on the way back, I saw the place lit up with bright and vibrant lights as the sky fades to black. It was as if I was in space, surrounded by the stars.

Eventually I had made it home, and despite it being quite a rough day with school and all, I did find some peace in the calmness of the creek. Seeing the beauty of it, not only in the day time, but especially in the night time. And as I pack and arrange my stuff, for yet another day at school tomorrow. I went to sleep peacefully, as I pictured the image of those bright lights in the night time.

Under Pressure

The following day at school, it was the same thing as usual. Going through the same seven subjects the whole day. Doing countless classworks, topped up with a bag of homework to do when we get home. So, I was basically just busy working on school work the whole day, well, apart from our thirty minute break in the middle of the day. That's really the only time where I can just have a laugh with my friends, as we eat our snacks. Other than that, it's just finishing assignments, answering a bunch of quizzes and tests, and making sure I complete all the homework given on that day before I go to bed.

It's a very drooling process, I mean half of the time you'll find me falling asleep while doing the assignments and getting up three or four hours later. But oh well, I had to do that for me to even get an average grade. And this carried on, from first grade till the eight grade.

I mean, apart from the expectations that my parents had for me, there was also some self-pressure that played a role in me being so eager to get things done properly as soon as possible. Because I didn't want to let any of them down, let alone let myself down as well.

But I guess, that prolonged period of self pressure and stress got the better of me. Seeing as I had multiple white hairs on my head, when I was just twelve years of age. From there on, I've been called an old man of the class and many other things. But you know, it is what it is. I mean, I didn't give myself much of a choice now did I. But I guess, it's worth it in a sense that, up till now I've been very keen on being on time and getting things done on time as well. So at least I learned to be punctual.

Losing Time

In the next few days, I've noticed that days were getting shorter and shorter. It was as if the twenty four hours that we usually have in a day, was simply cut by half. It was so weird, it was like time began to suddenly speed up. Where I was seeing seconds turn to minutes, minutes turn to hours, and hours turn to days. I would usually expect this to happen, whenever I'm busy doing something, or whenever I'm out with my family or friends. But this time, time is just casually passing by, even when I'm just sitting and staring at the clock. I thought that maybe I was just seeing things, or maybe it was just all in my head. But it wasn't.

Sooner or later, I saw my family and friends questioning how fast time was moving as well. So, this is really happening huh? Time just suddenly decided to speed up. Sure, It shocked me at first, but I didn't really feel the effect of it. Everything was still the same, I was still going to school, going out with my family, hanging out with my friends, and I was still doing loads of school work. My life was pretty much as it was, even before I noticed time moving so fast.

But I was completely proven wrong the following weeks. I started to notice that as I was going on with my usual routine. I was starting to miss out on certain tasks, assignments, or just general things that I would usually do in a day. And before I go to bed, I would wonder and ask myself, did I complete that task that I was supposed to do? Did I forget anything today?, and I usually end up missing something. So, I would get out of bed and try to complete whatever it is that I missed, and then go to bed. I noticed that hangouts and conversations with my friends have gone by faster. We could literally just be catching up, and then we'd see that three to five hours have already gone by. Experiencing this, had me questioning whether I would really have enough time to do all the things I set out to do.

In The Blink of An Eye

As I was once again in that stage of procrastinating and overthinking, my mind and heart were spiraling out of control. Being overwhelmed by so many thoughts and emotions. Thoughts and emotions that only continued to add onto the pressure and stress that I was already feeling, simply trying to cope with all the things that I had to take care of in regards to my personal life, my academics, my relationships with my friends and families as well. I was just jumbling a ton of things all at once, and it was far from convenient or easy. Seeing as jumbling everything all at once, caused me to miss out on hangouts with my friends, outings with my family, high school experiences and events, and assignments and projects as well.

From a twelve year old, who was so sure of what he wanted to do in life, to a thirteen year old who's got all of these different things that he has to do. Things and tasks that aren't even supposed to be in his so-called "plan". His journey escalated for the worst, in the span of a single year. At this point, I am a complete mess. The only time I could ever have for me to just stop for a second and breathe, is when I go to the creek. But that alone only lasts for about thirty minutes to an hour. Then it's back to that hell of a phase again. It's like a torturous cycle that never seems to end, no matter how far I get.

I mean I had karate classes on friday, just so that I could defend my weak self against bullies and all that. Then I had to go to church on saturday, so I was basically fully booked most of, if not all the time. I tried praying to God, for some guidance or signs to let me know if what I'm doing right now will be all worth it. If the things that I am doing are helping me in finding out what path I must walk in this life. I even asked if God could just show me my path in life, so that I could just pursue it head on already. Instead of constantly running into these intersections, that just continues to redirect me to another path, time and time again. So, I've waited, and waited, and waited. But sadly, I never got an answer.

Chapter III

The Stage Of Doubt

Completely Derailed

The more time seems to go by, the more I seem to lose it. The more I tried to focus on school, the more I seemed to hate it. The more I spent time with my friends, the more I got shouted at and insulted for it. The more I tried to please my family, the more I disappointed them, and every time I thought I was getting closer to achieving my dreams, the further they became. It's like whatever I do, no matter how much effort I put into it, no matter how much I try, I always end up failing. It's like life continues to just spit in my face, and knock me down every single time. Only for me to get back up, so that it could do it to me all over again.

I was never the most athletic, I was never good looking, I was never cool, I was never fun to be around, I was never the most talkative, I was never the most confident, I was never the most charming or enthusiastic. But for a second, I thought I could the smartest, but apparently that got taken away from me as well. I just could never win. It was as if all the odds were just stacked against me. And now, I'm nothing but a pathetic loser, who's faced with failures every single moment of my life. I'm just someone, who constantly regrets every single choice he's made up till now.

I was so discouraged, so let down, that I couldn't even look at myself in the mirror. I completely shut myself out from everyone. I didn't want to tell anyone about anything that was going on in my life. I stopped praying. I lost faith. I lost hope. I stopped talking. I stopped having fun. I stopped trying, and I stopped dreaming. All I was doing now, was simply existing.

An Emo Phase

I thought that I'd naturally be okay, with the passage of some time. Since they say that time heals all wounds right? But apparently, I was wrong yet again. Since months had passed and I still wasn't even close to being okay. I was still so discouraged and derailed that I spent most of my days, locked up in my room, in the dark, staring at completely nothing. Just thinking to myself, what the heck am I doing with my life. I was constantly replaying past failures, shortcomings, and mistakes, asking myself, what could I have done better?. But my mind came up with nothing but more questions, and depressing thoughts and conclusions. So, it was pretty much useless.

I wanted to shut myself out from the world and everyone in it so badly that I'd have my headphones on, as I just listen to music at max volume. Just so that I'd be taken out of reality for a while. But that didn't help, it just added to the pain. So, I was just basically torturing myself, and for some odd reason I was okay with it. I was apparently completely fine with sobbing for hours on end, while listening to old love songs, and that was just at home. In school it was a whole different, I was doing stupid stuff, fooling around, and trying to take fights when anyone would pick on me. You could say that I was a ticking time bomb at this point, just waiting to explode.

I became careless, I was tripping and falling down more than usual. I scraped my arms and feet, and got a few bumps on my head as well. Which is why I have so many scars on my body. I hated myself so much that I didn't care whether I got hurt or not. I didn't care if I got more bruises and wounds, I didn't care if I bled. You could say that I completely disregarded my well-being physically, mentally, emotionally, and spiritually all together. I was basically telling the world that I didn't care whether I die or not. And whenever someone would ask me if I was okay, I would just constantly reply with the same answer that all of us reply with, when we don't really want to tell anyone about how much pain we're in. The famous two words known as, "I'm fine".

Silent

Silent is what I've become, when it comes to my worries. Silent is what I've become, when it comes to my problems. Silent is what I've become, when it comes to my emotions. Silent is what I've become, when it comes to my thoughts. Silent is what I've become as a person. I no longer spoke to anyone, unless I was spoken to. I no longer opened up about myself, unless I was asked. And even when I decided to open up, I usually gave very vague answers. I was never really fond of letting anyone know the whole story of what's going on in my life, let alone in my life as well. But at the same time, I just knew deep down that they wouldn't really be interested in getting to know the whole story. And even if they were, I'm pretty sure at some point, they were going to start judging me, painting this perception that they have of me, simply based on my thoughts, emotions, or what I was going through. I mean, it's bad enough that I already felt quite derailed myself, I don't need another person or multiple people making me feel even more derailed and depressed.

So, I was there to do whatever I asked to do and nothing else. When I was at school, all I did was the classwork and homework. I would still hangout with my friends but it didn't feel the same. I mean, all I really did was look at them having fun, laughing and smiling, as they all goofed around. At times, when they did try to include me in the fun, I would just say, "It's okay, I'll just eat" or "You guys go ahead" with a little smile. Just to cover up the pain that I was feeling. When I was at home, I would just go up to my room and shut the door, as I listened to songs at high volume in the dark. I would only come out when I had homework to do, or if I was called to eat, but those were really the only times where I would really come out. And even when it was breakfast, lunch, or dinner, I was just there eating, not talking or looking at anything else but my food. And as everyone began sharing about how their day went, and how they were feeling, I just sat there eating, and gave the occasional smile. When they had asked me how my day went, I would always give them the usual "it was good", and if they asked me how I was feeling, I would just say that I'm fine, with a smile. Just to hide all the pain, anxiety, stress, sorrow, and anger that I was feeling. So, there I was. A guy who just sits in the corner, all alone, silently sulking in his sorrows, and failures, as time continues to just pass him by.

Slowly Killing Me

I didn't notice it at first. But as time went by, I started to feel weaker and weaker with every passing day. At first it was my mind, I began to forget things more often. I would be needing to go to the kitchen to get a pack of chips, and three minutes later when I'm already at the kitchen, I would forget the reason as to why I came to the kitchen in the first place. Instances like this would happen every single time from then onwards, and it still continues to happen up till today. I mean, I can't even count the amount of times where I've forgotten where I've kept certain things, forgotten plans that I had made with my friends so that we could hangout, forgotten about family plans, forgotten about assignments that I had to do, and the list goes on and on. Then it started affecting my emotions, where I would feel sad and down out of nowhere, even though nothing bad happened. There are even times where I would feel completely exhausted to do anything, even though I had just woken up.

There are times where I would just have these constant changes in my mood. I could literally be so happy one minute, and the next minute I would begin to feel extremely angry, sad, or irritated. It was as if my body didn't want me to feel any positive feelings for a prolonged period of time. Since I would instantly revert back to being depressed, with the blink of an eye. Then it began to affect my body physically. I would get these chest pains, and headaches out of nowhere one day, and then the next day they're gone. Then, after a while they would return, and it always happened whenever I felt sad, hurt, anxious, or angry. I was literally dying inside, not knowing what to make of all of these pains, and constant shifts in emotions and thoughts. I didn't know if it was serious or not, I didn't know if this was real, or if it's just all in my head, I didn't know if this was normal or if I was going insane. I just didn't know what to do, and I was so scared to ask anyone for help. So, I just dealt with it myself.

Tough Luck

As I continued to deal with these emotions and thoughts by myself, I noticed that nobody cares. Nobody really cares whether you're going through a hard time. Nobody cares whether you're in pain. Nobody cares whether you're slowly falling apart. Nobody cares if you're in tough situations. Noticing this made me realize that nobody truly cares about anyone else but themselves. People just make you feel like they care for you in the moment, but as time goes on and as you continue to face a lot of adversities. You'll start to notice that the amount of people, who said that they'll be there for you, who said that they'll continue to support you, who said that they'll help you when you're in trouble, begin to slowly disappear. Till eventually, you're just left with yourself, and if you're lucky, you'll still have a few people left.

I mean, it's understandable. Everyone's got their own problems and issues to deal with right?. I mean, with what the world's becoming right now, it's no wonder everyone's so self conscious and self centered. I mean there are people who are depressed, suicidal, and struggling with their mental health as well, in a world that so driven by success, achievements, and money. No wonder, there are many instances of unfair practices, cheating, and people taking advantage of each other, just to get what they want. Everyone just wants to be at the top, everyone just wants to be the best, and at times they don't even care about how many people they hurt, cheat, or lie to. As long as they get what they want, they're fine with it. I found it to be very disappointing and quite vile.

But the worst part that I've noticed is that, if you're one of the people who's kind, caring, trusting, helpful, smart, compassionate, and fair, you will rarely win or succeed. But what's a guarantee, is that more people will approach you, befriend you, get close to you, only to use you, take advantage of you, and then leave you, when they finally get what they want from you. But wait, it doesn't end there, because they'll come back to you, only to do the same thing over and over again. It's a vicious, and draining cycle that all of us will experience at some point of our lives. And it just flat out sucks.

A Slap In The Face

I was bashed for being at the top. I was insulted and unmotivated, when I was at the bottom. I was told to be sad and disappointed, whenever I was satisfied and happy with my work. I was told that I was worthless, when I had a glimpse of confidence in myself. I was called weak, whenever I cried or talked about how I felt. But I was shouted at and insulted, for being strong, and acting like nothing's wrong. I was told to focus and prioritize myself. But when I did, I was called selfish and inconsiderate. I was told to be kind, I was told to help others when they asked for help. But when I was asking for help, nobody even bothered to offer a helping hand. I was told to support and care for my loved ones, in the things that they love to do. But nobody cares and supports me, when it comes to things I love to do. I was told to love with all my heart, but when I did she just left me for someone else. My loved ones told me to dream big, and go after my dreams. But when I did, they were the ones who were trying to stop me.

All of this sounds like the most hypocritical things I've ever heard, and it is. Never in my life have I ever seen or heard something like this. I guess this is the main reason as to why I hate myself so much. It's not because I've failed or made mistakes. It's not because I couldn't achieve my dreams. It's because I believed in and allowed these stupid opinions and insults dictate my choices in life. It's because I allowed these idiotic claims, and words, to ruin my life. I basically allowed everyone and everything to constantly slap me in the face, over and over again. Not giving myself a say in what I wanted to do, or what I wanted out of my life. I just listened to all of these people, thinking that they knew what's best for me. But in the end, all it brought me was pain, sorrow, stress, and a boat load of regret.

Regretful & Rageful

Upon realizing the ugly truth, I grew rageful with every passing day. Constantly reliving life choices that I've made, with a lingering feeling of regret. Knowing that I could've done so much better, if I'd just listened to my gut, instead of listening to everyone else's opinions. I began to have this excruciating pain in my chest day in and day out. But this time, it just wouldn't go away. No matter how much I try to forget about it, it always comes back to haunt me. I just wanted to shout it all out, at the top of my lungs, I wanted to curse at everyone so badly, I wanted to let them all know how selfish and unfair they've been. But I didn't, because they just wouldn't care. They'd just take it in, and forget about it the very next minute like nothing ever happened, or worse, they would just say that it was all my fault and they had nothing to do with it.

So, I did the only thing that I could do, and that was to continue being alone. I started on going on long walks around the creek again, from the afternoon up till the night. I started writing more, seeing as that was my only outlet. It was the only way that I could say what I wanted to say. And so, I would write and write and write, until my hands ached, until I had no pages to write on anymore. There were instances where I would even spend the whole day, just writing. I've probably written hundreds, if not thousands of poems on sorrow, heartbreak, and pain. I mean, I've tried doing so many other things, to try to help me cope with my anger, but none of them really helped. This was the only way that I could find some sort of comfort or peace, in this whirlwind of insecurities, doubts, rage and regrets.

Chapter IV

Finding My Path

Could This Be Real?

Fast forward to four years later, I'm seventeen years of age, I've gotten a little taller, and I've gained some weight. Oh, and I'm in university now, and I've gone into business as my course, seeing as I pretty much didn't have any other choice. But those are the only things that have changed. Other than that, I'm still pretty much the same bitter, regretful, and rageful person. Only this time, I'm smiling a lot more. I can still remember that day like it was yesterday. I had made my way to the university lounge. Feeling worried, yet somewhat optimistic that this phase of my life wouldn't be as bad as the past phases that I've experienced in my life so far. I mean I've started it out pretty well. I approached and got to know a couple pretty awesome people, and went to some pretty sick and crazy parties too. If I'm being honest, my foundation year in university was one of the best parts of my life. I was feeling free, I was feeling happy, I was so positive, and all in all, I was just enjoying life, even though I still haven't figured out the path I wanted to take.

This helped me in a way, in forgetting all the horrific moments that I've had. All the feelings of sorrow and regret, that I've lingered on for quite a long time. It was like the feeling of being high up in the clouds again, you know, where everything is just so bright and clear. I wasn't planning for the future, I wasn't dwelling in the past, I was just focused on the present, what was happening right here, right now. Sure, it wasn't all rainbows and sunshine, but despite the roadblocks, despite the tears that I've cried, despite the failures, despite the setbacks, despite the struggles and problems that I've encountered along the way. I was still able to smile, and figured out how to get through that tough situation. It's so crazy as I think about it, since for once, I actually allowed myself to have fun again, to connect with people again, to enjoy life again, and to be happy again.

It felt so surreal, that everyday when I get home and go to bed, I keep asking myself whether any of this was actually real. I thought that every single day was just some amazing fantasy that was all in my head. But every single day that I wake up, I'm reminded that all of this is real. And knowing that, every single morning of every single day, just continued to put a big old smile on my face.

The Life Of A Business Student

I had never thought that I would ever in my wildest dreams pursue the field of business. But I guess that there's a first time for everything right?. Well, now that you've got an insight on how the fun side of university life is, let me tell you about the stressful, and at times boring side of it. For starters, there is an extremely annoying amount of math that is involved. Well, I suppose that is expected. Seeing as we're dealing with money after all. So yeah, there's a lot of calculations and computations to be done in each class. Especially in one of the courses, which is named Business Mathematics. So yeah, I'd never thought I would be best friends with a calculator, but here we are.

Apart from all the math involved, there's also a lot of presentations to be done. Luckily for me, I was already able to do presentations on pretty much any topic, thanks to high school. But what I was not looking forward to is the dress code that we have to follow whenever we were doing presentations. I had to wear ties, polos, slacks, and dress shoes. I mean, that just screamed uncomfortable to me back then, and that's not even the worst part. What's worse was wearing all of that, and walking under the blazing hot sun. Imagine taking the time and effort to look so well groomed, and smart, and then having it all ruined by sweat stains. It's as if all your effort was taken away in the span of a few minutes.

So there's that. Oh, and don't get me started on the tests and group projects. Those raised my stress levels to the roof. Imagine solving twenty to fifty math problems, which require an unreasonable amount of steps for you to get just one answer. As for the group projects, oh man that's another story. You've got to deal with your groupmates being late, their issues and problems, their questions, their inconsistencies, and their mistakes, on top of your own. Especially when you're the group leader. Your group mates will be looking to you for your answers, for solutions, and for guidance. And you must have the answers to all of their questions, or else it will be a complete catastrophe. It's pressure that could make anyone's hair easily turn white. I mean, you can take me as an example. I was only seventeen at the time, and I already had a head filled with white hair.

So yeah, in a nutshell, business people are stressed out, yet organized, calculated, and presentable human beings. And I was on the path to becoming one.

Trying to Enjoy The Process

Although I never really saw myself becoming a businessman, nor have I thought of even doing it for a living, I had to learn to deal with it. Imagine that, someone like me, enjoying a life that constantly involves calculating the profit gained and lost by a business, the total amount of revenue needed by a company; in order for them to obtain the necessary resources for their business to succeed. But unfortunately for me, I had to learn to enjoy all of the rigorous processes and tasks. Well, that took a very long time, and I mean a very very long time. As it would take me days to complete an assignment from our courses. I would spend hours, stressing myself out. As I constantly try to calculate the answers to these questions from my assignment. I was always on the edge of my seat whenever I would come up with an answer. Since I have to recheck my steps and calculations, and if they don't align with the answers given in the textbooks, I would have to redo the whole thing all over again.

So, I needed to be darn near perfect in my assignments. Otherwise, I would have to suffer through another hour or two of painful and brain numbing calculations. As you can imagine, I was far from perfect and I did have to redo most of the tasks and assignments. But the feeling, oh the feeling of finally getting right, was immensely satisfying. It's like every time I got it right, it was as if I'd won the lottery or something. Well, now you know just how much I hate math. But as for the presentations, it wasn't really that bad. I already knew how to present certain topics to an audience, make sure you look at the audience while presenting, make sure to interact with the audience as well while presenting, as well as back up plans such as, how to recover or get back to the topic if you get lost, and that is simply by looking at the slide. I mean, I've pretty much got the basics down, it was just the preparation for the presentation which was a little stressful having to understand boatloads of information relating to business, the external and internal factors that affect it, customer relationship management, profitability of a business, and so and so forth. So yeah, it required a lot of focus, practice, hard work, and brain power. But I managed to pull through, somehow.

How Did I Get Here?

Now you're probably thinking, how on earth did I go from wanting to become a rockstar, or a doctor, to a businessman? Well it all started, when I finished highschool. It was time for me to look for a university to apply to. Me and my best friend planned to enroll in the same university, so the two of us went university hunting during the summer. At the time, I planned to take up psychology, since I decided on becoming a therapist. Mainly because I found myself being fascinated by learning the how and why we think and feel as human beings, and I found myself wanting to help people with their emotional and mental problems or issues. As for my best friend he planned to take mechanical engineering, since he was very into physics and engineering.

So off we went, scouting and applying to universities around the city of Dubai. But unfortunately we weren't having any luck. Since they required such high qualifications and grades, our grades were pretty much average. Not to mention their fees. Oh man, I never knew that universities cost so much. I mean, you could literally buy an apartment, villa, or car, with that money. So, apart from their requirements, our other problem was trying to find a university which we could afford. Eventually, we stumbled upon this university near my best friend's place. It was affordable, our grades fit their requirements, and it was near the metro, it was perfect, or so we thought. So we applied, and a few days later we got a call back from the university. Sadly, it was bad news, they said that apparently they required higher grades than what we had. So, they rejected our application.

My best friend and I were completely shocked and disappointed. We went home, and relayed the bad news to our parents. His dad decided to enroll him for a job training in the culinary field, so there was that. As for me, I had a talk with my parents. They asked me what I wanted to take, and I replied saying Psychology, because I wanted to become a therapist. But my parents weren't really into the idea of that, so they recommended me to take business management. SInce they wanted me to follow in the footsteps of my dad. I tried bargaining and convincing them to let me take psychology, since I really liked it. But apparently not even my bargaining skills were enough to change their mind, and the fact that the only university that would accept me as a student in their university, despite my average grades, was a business university. And so, that is how I ended up here, studying a business course in a business university.

Not As Bad As I Expected To Be

As I continued doing this course, and dealing with all the work and stress that came with it, I still found myself enjoying each class, and having with my friends there whenever it was our free time. We would mostly spend our time around the lounge, playing foosball and ping pong. I could still remember those intense foosball games, against those 1st year students. Man, they were good, and I got to be good friends with them as well. I mean we still follow each other on instagram and chat every now and then till this day, so that's a good sign. As for me and my classmates, well considering that they were all smokers, we spent most of our time downstairs in the smoking area, near the parking lot. Oh man, that was our spot. That's where we would mess around, tell stupid stories about all the weird stuff we did, and so crazy dares as well. Then after university, we would always go to this shawarma shop nearby, and grab a bite. I even remember that we took turns to see who would be the one to treat the whole group.

As for the teachers, they were pretty cool as well. We had a teacher who was really athletic, I mean the guy played basketball every night after teaching. Then there was our other teacher, who was so fun, and she had us falling in love with her Brazilian accent. Oh man, she sounded so nice. They were all pretty chill with us as well, they'd let us finish our work on our own time, and didn't heckle us one bit. I mean, of course there were instances where they shouted and got pissed, because our class was too noisy at times. But other than those rare instances, we connected with them. They were so relatable to us, and they basically vibed with our way of thinking. That just made attending class, and learning these mundane topics more fun and interesting.

Overall, my foundation year in university was nothing short of a blast. I had fun, I made really cool friends, I met awesome and chill teachers. I became friends with the security guard, oh man that guy was cool. He was a bit scary the first time I met him, but as time went on we became cool with each other. So yeah, It was a fun first experience in university. But eventually, it had to end. Since we had to transfer due to the university changing its standards of what type of grades we needed to have in high school for us to continue in the university. We basically needed to have high grades. So, it was university hunting for me again.

Help From An Old Friend

As I was trying to look for a university that I could apply to, I stumbled upon an old friend of mine. She and I met during a choir practice, and so, seeing as we haven't spoken to or saw each other for quite a while, we decided to catch up. Apparently she's been doing really well, she's currently studying computing in this university that she enrolled in, which was really good. But anyways, she then asked me if I was in university and I replied saying that I was, but something happened and they didn't let us continue. It was right then and there, where she asked me to join their university. Since they were going to be having an open house in the coming week. So, I said "sure i'll check it out", and filled with joy she said, "alright cool, cool. See you then. Bye. Take care", as she went for her choir practice.

When I got home that day, I immediately told my mom about the news and she was glad that I found a new university to enroll in. So, a week passed by pretty quickly, and it was time to go to the open house. It was quite a long drive, since it was in another city. It took about an hour to get there. When I got there though, I immediately started talking and interacting with some other students there as well. You know, just trying to get to know my potential classmates and all. Then after probably half an hour, they called me up for registration. As I was making my way to the reception, I saw my friend from church. We said hey, and she introduced me to her friend who was a cool dude. He was studying computing as well. So yeah, I made a couple of friends, and when I went to the reception, I completed the submission of documents and registration. Then as I was about to leave the campus, the academic coordinator stopped and asked if I wanted to take the scholarship exam to get a discount on the fees. I said yes, since it was just multiple choice and the test was on basic english, math, and science. So, I did the test, and I miraculously passed and managed to score a seventy percent discount on the fees. And so, there was a month left before the first semester started. So, I had just got some rest, and got everything else in order for me to get started with university yet again.

The First Year

It was finally my first year in university. I was a young and driven mind entering a new environment. So, I had just done what I thought I was supposed to do, and introduced myself to one of my classmates as I entered the class. Eventually that classmate became a close friend of mine in university. We could hangout all the time, and I got to know a lot of awesome and wonderful people in my class as well. Well, up until the point where I got transferred to another batch because of my credentials I guess. So yeah, I was basically alone again. Well, not necessarily since I did know one person there in that new class, it was my sister's friend's elder sister, yeah I know it's confusing but yup she was the only one who I knew. So, she became one of my good friends as well. And it was through her that I got to know all of our other classmates and a lot of other cool people as well in the university. This was also the first time where I decided to start selling my writings. So, I created a book called "Poems of Love" and I was able to sell a few copies to my friends. And one of the very first people to buy my first book was my sister's friend's elder sister, so that was pretty cool.

But study wise, well teachers were still cool. They were quite friendly, relatable, and fun to be around. Some of the lectures, though, got a bit too repetitive and boring at times. But overall, the assignments were pretty new and creative. I mean, we got to create our very own resume or CV in the form of a video, so there's that. But as you may know by now, my life is always filled with challenges, drawbacks and failures. So, there was this one course, where I was struggling. It was called managing data, and we were basically learning how to calculate costs through formulas in excel, and create charts and data tables for analysis of information such as financials of a company and so on. So, I struggled with that for a while. I was having trouble getting formulas and table structures right. I think it's safe to say that I've failed a couple of times, but in the end I managed to pull through, pass the exam, and move on to year two.

The Second Year

Well, unfortunately my second year in university was completely online due to the pandemic. So, I was pretty much stuck at home, just watching my teacher explain the topic for the day on google meet, like it was a youtube video. As for my classmates, well, all of us had our cameras on so at least I could see them as well, and despite it being online, everyone still had the same energy as they had in class, so it wasn't all that different. But little did I know, that in the following weeks to come that would all change, and it would eventually get much more boring. And it did, little by little as time went on, classes started to feel like you're watching a video instead of a live teaching session. Since everyone, slowly started closing their cameras, muting their mics completely, leaving the call, and so on. I was the only one left, with a camera on and who was the only one who was participating in class as well. So, it got quite lonely and boring if I'm being honest.

But I guess the bright side to everything being online, was that it made it much easier and convenient for us to complete our assessments and projects. Seeing as we were all just at home, we had all the time in the world to properly do and complete our projects and assessments. It also gave me time for writing poems and books that I would soon continue to publish online through amazon. So yeah, despite the repetitive and boring nature that comes with being locked in your house. There are still some bright sides to it as well. But anyways, our university decided to host online events as well, like esports, short film contests, online quizzes, and so on. So, that made it quite interesting, since I participated in both esports and the short film contests. And now, I'm guessing that you're wondering whether I won or not, well, our team won in esports, but I lost in the short film contest. Nonetheless, despite me losing, I went away with a new hobby. So, time went by extremely fast actually, despite us just being at home all day. And before I knew it, it was already summer break.

A Social Media Marketer

Over the summer, I thought of applying for a job. Seeing as my classmates were doing part time jobs during the semester as well, and they were getting paid a pretty good amount of money. So, I thought to myself, why don't I apply for a job as well. I mean, I'm pretty much free for the summer, so I might as well use the time to earn some money so that I could possibly pursue a publishing deal that I've been putting aside for quite a while because of the lack of money, and gain some real work experience as well, while I'm at it. So I applied for multiple jobs in the field of social media marketing, seeing as that is something that I could do, since I already have an idea about social media and marketing.

So after weeks of constantly applying to jobs, and getting rejected. One company called Sinatra Holdings, finally accepted my application for an internship in social media marketing. So, I went for the interview, and I was very early. You know, first impressions are everything, so I wanted to make a good one. Anyways, at the interview I was asked to create a marketing strategy for a beauty salon, so I just spewed a couple of ideas on creating video reels, posting pictures, and creating behind the scenes videos to post on the beauty salon's social media pages, along with relevant hashtags and captions to go with it. Just so that the general audience would be aware of their services and products that they offer. Then, after a few more questions, I eventually got the job and I started right away.

I was basically in charge of creating and managing their social media pages for their company's businesses. So, I would be in charge of coordinating with their content writers and designers to come up with enticing content for their pages. It was a pretty nice job, a bit hectic and stressful at times but it was alright. I liked the people, they were very accommodating and easy to get along with. I did mess up a lot at work, but I was able to bounce back and do better next time. And eventually, I did gain some knowledge on what it's like to manage and promote a company's services and products on social media. At last the internship was coming to an end, since the job was only for three months and university was starting again as well. So, I bid farewell to all my colleagues there at that company, and went back to university.

The Third Year

I was in my third year in university, I was finally the senior. I couldn't believe how time just flew by so fast. It was almost as if, all of this just happened in the blink of an eye. But anyways we were given our new schedules, along with our new courses as well. But I would say that this year was by far the most challenging year among the bunch. I mean apart from the courses being much harder and lengthier, I was also given the responsibility of being the class leader. So, once again I had everybody else's problems, concerns, and issues in my head on top of my own. I had to pretty much handle my own problems and find solutions for it, as well as handle other people's problems and help them find a solution to all of their problems too. This was probably the only year, where I had more than ten notifications ringing on my phone, every single day. All of it was my classmates, asking me for stuff and help on our courses and university in general.

I had to deal with a lot of redo's and adjustments to my assessments and projects. Since they were either lacking something, or needing a bit more clarification in certain areas. Apart from that, well, there were also some problems with the teachers and the briefs that were given for our assessments and projects, a lot of extensions in terms of deadlines for the assessments constantly requested by my classmates. Group projects going haywire, because of certain problems and circumstances that have risen, that weren't really doing good. A lot of conflict between management, teachers, and students, as well. It was a complete disaster, and that was only in the first semester. But despite all of that, I still don't know how, but we all managed to submit our assessments and projects on time, pass and do well in it as well. So, at least there was still a bright side to all of this.

A Job In Sales

In the middle of our first semester a friend of ours posted this job offer in class group chat. It was for this job in sales, for an IT Solutions company. The job was basically to call clients and sell them a QR Code Menu for restaurants and cafes. I decided to apply, so I sent my CV to my friend's email, and in a few days time I was called for an interview. It was on the day where we had class, luckily it was online though. So, I left class a little bit early, and ran since I was already running late. I got even more late, since I couldn't find the building and so I called up my friend and asked for directions. Eventually, I was able to find it, and made my way up to their office. When I reached there, I was sweating and hyperventilating, and I saw another friend of mine from church. Turns out, he was working there as well. But anyways I got on with the interview, and was asked if I did anything related to sales before, and I said that I never had any experience with sales, then I was asked a few more questions about my background, and so on and so forth. And eventually, as the interview came to a close, I got the job. And I started on that very day itself as well.

So, I was basically tasked to just generate leads for my colleagues, listen and take note of whenever my friends would call and pitch to the clients. And I did that for a few weeks, and then I did some practice calls as well as with my manager, which were very intimidating and stressful. I was honestly having a really difficult time at first, where I couldn't get any of the info regarding the pitch correct. I was constantly making little mistakes, and forgetting key points to the pitch as well and I had instances where my mind just totally blacked out. I was a mess, I thought that I wouldn't be able to do this job, or that this line of work just wasn't for me. But as time went on, I kept practicing and taking into account the pointers and tips that my friends and manager gave me. I slowly began to learn and progressed, and when the time came for me to do my final practice call with my manager, I was so nervous. But in the end, I pulled it off. From there onwards, I was making call after call, after all, but I wasn't able to book any meetings. So, I went back to the drawing board, and took into consideration more tips and tricks that my friends were doing. And after some weeks of constant calling and improving my pitch I was able to book my first meeting. I was so relieved and happy, and from there onwards I just kept calling, and tried to learn new ways to improve my pitch and the way I spoke to the clients, and eventually booking meetings with clients became much more natural for me. And with a lot of time, patience, and hustle, I was able to close a few deals as well.

Which brings us to this very day. As of now, I'm still currently in university, doing my second semester in my third year. I'm still working in sales for the same company up till now, and I do plan to continue to work with them in the future as well. I'm still writing poems and stories, posting them on my facebook page, and publishing them on Amazon. Ever since my second year in university I've started a podcast on instagram and youtube, and I still continue to do it, till this very day. I'm still creating and posting short films as well on instagram and youtube too. Although I'm not an official author yet, I haven't really achieved any of the dreams that I've set out to achieve yet, although I still make mistakes, and although I'm still imperfect. One thing's for sure, I do have a path, and it's this very journey that I've been on, and will continue to go on for as long as I live. And although I'm not exactly where I want to be right now, I have faith that someday, I'll achieve every single thing I'd set out to do, and I'll be exactly where I'm supposed to be. At the very end of this journey.

The End